LATINOS IN BASEBALL

Manny Ramirez

Charlie Vascellaro

Mitchell Lane Publishers, Inc.
P.O. Box 200
Childs, MD 21916-0200

LATINOS IN BASEBALL

Tino Martinez	Bobby Bonilla	Roberto Alomar	Pedro Martinez
Moises Alou	Sammy Sosa	Ivan Rodriguez	Bernie Williams
Ramon Martinez	Alex Rodriguez	Vinny Castilla	**Manny Ramirez**

Library of Congress Cataloging-in-Publication Data

Vascellaro, Charlie
    Manny Ramirez / Charlie Vascellaro.
        p. cm. — (Latinos in baseball)
    Includes index.
    Summary: A biography of the power-hitting outfielder for the Cleveland Indians, from his childhood in the Dominican Republic and New York City through his days in the minor leagues to his major league debut and beyond.
    ISBN 1-58415-020-3
    1. Ramirez, Manny, 1972—Juvenile literature. 2. Baseball players—Dominican Republic—Biography—Juvenile literature. 3. Cleveland Indians (Baseball team)—Juvenile literature. [1. Ramirez, Manny, 1972- 2. Baseball players.] I. Title. II. Series.
GV865.R38 V28 2000
796.357'092—dc21
    [B]   99-054106

About the Author: Charlie Vascellaro is the Director of Public Relations for Maryland Baseball, LLC, which owns and operates the Baltimore Orioles minor-league affiliate Bowie Baysox, Frederick Keys, and Delmarva Shorebirds. A freelance writer, Mr. Vascellaro's work has appeared in the *Arizona Republic* newspaper, the *New York Yankees* and the *Arizona Diamondbacks* magazines, and other major-league team magazines. He has also worked for the Arizona State University, coordinating the Diamonds in the Desert International Baseball Conference. He lives in Annapolis, Maryland.

Photo Credits: cover: Photo File; p. 4 Harry How/Allsport; pp. 14, 18 Steve Mandl; p. 31 Photo File; p. 33 Jim Commentucci/Allsport; p. 37 Craig Jones/Allsport; p. 39 Photo File; p. 43 Rick Stewart/Allsport; p. 47 Ron Kuntz/Archive Photos; p. 48 Allsport; p. 51 David Ceelic/Allsport; p. 54 Ezra Shaw/Allsport; p. 58 Ron Kuntz/Archive

Acknowledgments: The following story has been thoroughly researched and checked for accuracy. To the best of our knowledge, it represents a true story. However, this story is neither authorized nor endorsed by Manny Ramirez or any of his representatives. The author's sincerest appreciation goes to Tim Wiles at the National Baseball Hall of Fame Library in Cooperstown, New York; Steve Gietschier, archivist at the *Sporting News*; and Steve Mandl at George Washington High in New York for their cooperation.

TABLE OF CONTENTS

Chapter 1   Excitement in New York 5

Chapter 2   The Dominican 9

Chapter 3   Coming to America 13

Chapter 4   Becoming a Pro 17

Chapter 5   Triumph and Tragedy 24

Chapter 6   First Big Year 32

Chapter 7   Keeping Pace With Himself ... 41

Chapter 8   The Year of the Home Run 50

Chapter 9   Top Run Producer 56

Chronology   62

Major-League Stats 63

Index   64

CHAPTER ONE
Excitement in New York

"*M ami, ya me subieron a las grandes ligas,*" the young Dominican-born outfielder said when he called his mother with the news. "Mommy, they called me up to the major leagues."

Manny Ramirez had played in his first major-league game, for the Cleveland Indians, the night before in Minnesota. He was still an unknown rookie, and did not get a hit in four times at bat. He had just recently joined the Indians after playing exceptionally well for two of their minor-league farm teams earlier in the season. Two days later he was in New York, his second hometown, where he had grown up and played baseball since he was 12.

Just about anyone who has ever attended a major-league baseball game can still recall the overwhelming feeling of entering a big-league ballpark for the very first time: the brilliant green of the perfectly trimmed grass; the vast expanse of the outfield and the awe-inspiring size of the stadium itself; the amazing ability of the players hitting and catching the ball even during batting practice; and the tremendous roar of the crowd after the game begins. Entering a major-league ballpark for the first time is so exciting it can be frightening. Down on the field, young players often have the same overwhelming feelings the first time they walk onto a major-league diamond.

From the baseball field he played on at George Washington High School, in the Dominican-immigrant neighborhood of Washington Heights, Manny could see the lights of Yankee Stadium, where he dreamed of playing someday. Manny Ramirez was a 21-year-old rookie outfielder playing for the Cleveland Indians when he entered Yankee Stadium in the Bronx, New York, for the first time as a ballplayer on September 2, 1993. Yankee Stadium is one of the country's oldest and most famous ballparks. And for those whose dreams come true, they never forget their first game at Yankee Stadium.

Along with the thousands of fans who filled Yankee Stadium that night were about 50 of Manny Ramirez's friends and family who came to see him play.

"I'm excited about that," Manny said to a reporter earlier in the day.

His heart must have been beating loud and fast as the sights and sounds of Yankee Stadium surrounded him. His friends and family had been waiting for this day since he arrived in their neighborhood and began playing baseball eight years before. Manny's school-mates, neighbors and relatives formed a loud cheering section for him in Yankee Stadium that night.

"He's taking all of us with him," said Ralph Gonzalez, the first baseman from Manny's high-school team. "He's putting Washington Heights on the map."

Manny had been away from home for two years, and after he called his mother the big news spread quickly throughout the neighborhood. Before the game Manny met with his friends where they used to hang out, at Las Tres Marias restaurant at 170th Street and Amsterdam Avenue, for his old usual pregame meal of steak and fried plantains.

"I miss my friends," he said. "I miss my food."

Washington Heights had always been Yankees territory, but now baseball fans like local mailman Pedro Sosa were wearing Indians hats for Manny.

"I'm shivering," said 22-year-old Sosa outside of a neighborhood market. "I feel like I'm making it too. How could I be jealous of him? We're all out there with him," he said, echoing the statements of Ralph Gonzalez. "We're so proud."

A group of young boys had gathered at the video arcade and game room next door, where a glass display case featured 23 different Manny Ramirez baseball cards.

"I never saw him play, but I heard he's a great player," an 11-year-old boy named Michael Tubens told a reporter from *The New York Times*. "They say he's one of the best. I got his autograph."

Michael was surprised that Manny was so approachable at the restaurant.

"It was like meeting a regular person," he said.

With the hours until game time racing by, Manny became eager for the game to begin and anxious to do something on the field for his friends and family.

"It was unbelievable," Manny said. "I remember it felt so funny in here [his stomach], like a butterfly."

Manny soon overcame his feelings, hitting a double that bounced over the wall in his first at bat. He was so excited he thought it was a home run and kept on running. His teammates teased him about his "rookie" mistake, but Manny had the last laugh twice, hitting a home run the second time he came to the plate—and another one after that! The first two hits came on pitches thrown by Yankees pitcher Melido Perez, who was also born in the Dominican Republic. In all, Manny drove in three runs and scored three as the Indians beat the Yankees 7-3.

"I just wanted to get a hit because all my friends were here," Manny told reporters after the game. "I wanted to look good for them. They pump me up."

Although there would still be many bumps in the road along the way (he did not get another hit in his next 17 times at the plate), Manny's big first night at Yankee Stadium was truly a sign of things to come.

"Making it to the major leagues is not the big thing," Manny told reporters the day of his big-league debut. "The big thing is how long you stay there—that's the problem."

CHAPTER TWO
The Dominican

For more than a hundred years, baseball has provided a way for waves of immigrants to become familiar with American culture. However, this is not the case for those coming to the Untied States from the Dominican Republic, where baseball has been acknowledged as the country's national game for almost as long as it has been in the United States. In fact, while football, basketball, hockey, and other games have competed for the attention of American sports fans, baseball has remained the favorite sport and consuming passion of the Dominican Republic.

Manuel Aristides Ramirez was born May 30, 1972, in Santo Domingo, the capital city of the Dominican Republic, a country poor in dollars but rich in baseball. In fact, no country has provided more players to the major leagues per capita (percentage of the country's total population) than the Dominican Republic. In the last 20 to 30 years many Dominicans, such as Moises Alou (whose father and uncles also played in the major leagues), Sammy Sosa, and Pedro Martinez have become some of baseball's brightest stars.

Located between Cuba and Puerto Rico, the Dominican Republic shares the island of Hispaniola with its neighbor country, Haiti. Baseball was brought to the Dominican Republic by the small island nation of Cuba, located sixty miles from Hispaniola to the northwest. North American sailors, students and businessmen had introduced the game to Cuba in the late 19th century. Cubans who had learned about baseball during visits to the United States also helped spread knowledge of baseball when they returned home.

During the period of 1868-1878, Cuba was fighting a war for independence from Spain, and many Cubans left the country seeking safety in Hispaniola. Most of these Cubans had worked in the sugar industry, trading with countries like the United States. They brought with them an ability to continue conducting their business and a newly discovered knowledge of baseball.

In his book, *The Tropic of Baseball*, author Rob Ruck refers to Dominican reporter Cuqui Cordova as "the foremost chronicler of the Dominican passion." Cordova explained how the Cubans helped bring baseball to the Dominican Republic. "They were running from war and they came to the Dominican Republic to live. They wanted to work, not fight, and they established themselves here. And soon, those who stayed wanted to do more than work. They wanted to play."

The first two teams to play baseball in the Dominican Republic were organized by a pair of Cuban brothers who made their living as ironworkers in Santo Domingo. In 1891 they put together teams made up of a combination of Cuban immigrants and Dominicans, as well as some North Americans and even a German restaurant owner. Although the two teams were named after a Cuban river (El Cauto) and a beer factory (Cerveceria), they eventually would simply be called the Blues (Azules) and Reds (Rojos). The teams played their first game with a baseball given to them by a North American sailor in the same town of Santo Domingo, where Manny Ramirez would be born 80 years later.

From this humble beginning, the growth of baseball in the Dominican Republic was fueled by the increasing popularity of the Cuban game. Radio broadcasts and newspaper accounts of Cuban ballgames played a big part in popularizing baseball in the Dominican Republic.

During the early 1900s and especially through the 1920s and 1930s, baseball spread from Cuba to the Dominican Republic and to Puerto Rico as players traveled with greater frequency to play in these neighboring countries as well as North America. Although Jackie Robinson would not break Major League Baseball's color barrier until 1947, Dominican and Cuban players such as Tetelo Vargas and Martin Dihigo became stars in the American Negro Leagues.

By 1959, when Fidel Castro came to power and forever changed U.S. relations with Cuba, many Cuban-born players such as Minnie Minoso and Camilo Pascual had already become established major-league stars. In the years to follow, many future major-leaguers would also come from Cuba, Puerto Rico, and the Dominican Republic. Ozzie Virgil, who played every position except pitcher during his nine-year career, became the first Dominican to play in the major leagues in 1956. His son Ozzie, Jr., would break into the big leagues in 1980. Other early Dominican standouts include the Alou brothers, Matty, Felipe, and Jesus, who played in the same major-league outfield together for the San Francisco Giants in the 1960s, as well as Hall of Fame pitcher Juan Marichal.

By the time Manny Ramirez was born in 1972, dozens of Dominican players had made it to the major leagues, with many more on the way.

According to Mike Hargrove, Manny's first manager in Cleveland, Dominican-born outfielder George (Jorge) Bell was an early hero of Manny's. Bell made his major-league debut with the Toronto Blue Jays in 1981 and was named the American League's Most Valuable Player in 1987. Another Dominican-born outfielder, Raul Mondesi, just one year older than Manny, is another of Manny's heroes.

During the late 1970s and early 1980s, the small Dominican town of San Pedro de Macoris became famous for providing major-league teams with many of their starting shortstops. In 1986, there were seven big-league shortstops who originally played in San Pedro de Macoris: Alfredo Griffin/Oakland Athletics, Nelson Norman/Texas Rangers, Rafael Ramirez/Atlanta Braves, Rafael Belliard/Pittsburgh Pirates, Rafael Santana/New York Mets, Tony Fernandez/Toronto Blue Jays, and Jose Uribe/San Francisco Giants.

Both San Pedro de Macoris and Santo Domingo have become celebrated gateways to the major leagues.

In 1999, out of 750 active major-league players, there were 66 Dominican-born players and 155 Latin Americans overall. More than 600 players from Latin American countries have worn major-league uniforms.

CHAPTER THREE
Coming to America

I n 1985, Manny Ramirez and his three sisters left the Dominican Republic with their parents, arriving in New York City when Manny was 12.

Manny's family established their American residence in a Dominican-immigrant neighborhood in New York called Washington Heights. His father Aristides worked as a cabdriver, and his mother Onelcidad was a seamstress in a dress factory. Although the asphalt and concrete of New York City was decidedly different from the tropical island Manny knew as a kid, one thing remained the same. Just like back home, baseball was the common bond and primary focus of the people in Manny's new community. While Manny's new neighborhood had problems with crime, drugs, and gang violence, Manny was able to avoid trouble by keeping his mind on baseball. Years later Manny talked about Washington Heights with a reporter from *Baseball America* magazine.

"I couldn't ever go out when I was young, like I could in the Dominican Republic, because of the area," Manny said. "You could see the dealers on every street corner on the way to school." A street gang known as the Zulus were a constant presence in his neighborhood.

"They never really bothered me," Manny remembered. "I didn't have a problem with that. We were busy playing baseball. I didn't hang around with the wrong people. All my friends were involved with sports. That's why I play baseball."

He worked his way up playing in well-known neighborhood leagues like the Pablo Morales and Alex Ferreiras Little Leagues, where former teammates said he used to cry about being the team's benchwarmer. Manny remembered how hard it was in the beginning.

"I was the ninth batter; everybody used to laugh at me," Manny recalled after he had become the best player for the all-Dominican team at George Washington High School.

Manny Ramirez at bat during a game for George Washington High School in Washington Heights, New York. Manny hit .643 and was named New York Public School's "High School Player of the Year" in 1991.

So great was Manny's desire to succeed at baseball that he would wake up at 4:30 A.M. to run and practice before school. He practiced with his high-school team on weekday afternoons and played sandlot games on weekends in the nearby neighborhood of Brooklyn.

The passion for the game and the quality of the baseball being played in the Washington Heights neighborhood had become well established by the time Manny began attending high school. During his senior year, *The New York Times* ran a series of articles about Manny's team.

Soon the entire neighborhood came to know Manny, who had become the star third baseman and center fielder on his team, and quite possibly the best high-school baseball player in New York City.

"He's from our country," said a local restaurant owner. "He's from our neighborhood. He's our guy."

The hard work and devotion that Manny applied to his baseball practice and workout sessions helped establish him as a legitimate major-league prospect. Manny would make his morning run uphill on a half-mile long street, dragging an old car tire tied to a rope around his waist.

"Run, Manny, run!" said one of the neighborhood ladies who worked at the school cafeteria. "Keep on! Or I'm not going to give you lunch."

Manny's legend continued to grow, and major-league scouts began showing up for the games at George Washington High School. The neighborhood was brightened by the lights of television crews coming to Washington Heights to cover Manny's story.

Younger kids in the neighborhood were already looking up to Manny, like ten-year-old second baseman Henry Payano, who kept a photograph of Manny on top of the television set at home and tried to swing like Manny when he came to bat in his Little League games. Manny was even a source of inspiration for adult fans of his high-school team.

"Not everyone can be that talented," said one fan to a *New York Times* reporter. "When you're around someone that talented you feel like you're part of him. You get happy. At least somebody's making it. Somebody's looking forward to his life."

A professional baseball career is not guaranteed to every high-school prospect. Even the best players sometimes fail to advance. The game becomes harder and more challenging as players go to college and the minor leagues. It's important for high-school baseball players to balance the time spent on baseball with time spent studying. During his senior year, Manny's attendance in school was better than in previous years; he received passing grades and improved his English. In the Dominican neighborhood of Washington Heights it was easy to get by without understanding English, but Manny's world would very soon extend beyond New York City.

CHAPTER FOUR
Becoming a Pro

Manny finished his senior season with a .643 batting average and was named the New York Public Schools' High School Player of the Year for 1991. Although he considered going to college, a few weeks later he was selected by the Cleveland Indians as the thirteenth overall pick in the first round of the major league's free-agent draft, and signed his first professional contract for $285,000.

"I signed," Manny later told *Baseball America*. "This was what I wanted to do."

Joe DeLucca, the scout who signed him, told *The New York Times* that Manny's swing was so beautiful, so natural, and so powerful that one like it comes along only once in a very long time. It was evident even in high school that Manny would most likely play in the major leagues someday, but like most players his age, first he would be required to prove himself at the minor-league level. His first professional assignment would be with Burlington, North Carolina, of the rookie-level Appalachian League. Burlington was yet another new home for Manny, and for the first time in his life he was without his family.

"The toughest thing was getting away from home, getting used to that," Manny remembered, "when you are young and don't know anything about your new place and you miss your family and friends."

He may have been homesick, but once again baseball made him feel comfortable in his new place and he continued to excel. In 59 games at Burlington, Manny had a .326 batting average, with 19 home runs and 63 runs batted in, leading his league in home runs and RBIs. He hit two grand slams in one week, just a month after leaving high school! At the end of the season, he was named the Appalachian League's Most Valuable Player and its top prospect.

This photo of Manny was taken while he was in the minor leagues.

In 1992, Manny was promoted to Class-A Kinston of the Carolina League, where he hit 13 home runs with 63 RBIs in 80 games. During one hot streak, Manny drove in 47 runs in 47 games. However, with about half of the season left to play, Manny suffered an injury to his left hand that sidelined him for the rest of the season. Although he had seriously bruised his hand, he was healed in time to earn another promotion, to the Double-A level, starting the 1993 season at Canton of the Eastern League. Each new league also represented a move to another town and a new home, but baseball remained the stabilizing force and focus of young Manny's life, and he kept getting better. Manny improved his numbers in just about every category, knocking in 17 home runs with 79 RBIs in 89 games, raising his batting average to a league-leading .340 and being named to the Eastern League's post-season All-Star team. As impressive as Manny's abilities appeared, he insisted that his skills did not come easy.

"Hitting is hard," Manny said. "It's hard to do that kind of hitting at each level."

The 1993 season would see Manny earn two more promotions, the first to the Triple-A Charlotte Knights of the International League, where he would blast another 14 homers in just 40 games. He led all the minor leagues with 44 doubles and a .613 slugging percentage, and was named *Baseball America*'s Minor League Player of the Year. At Charlotte he played for manager Charlie Manuel, a well respected hitting instructor who would later become the hitting coach and manager for the Cleveland Indians. Manuel was so impressed by Manny's hitting at the time, he told *Baseball America*, "I just leave him alone."

While 1993 was a memorable breakthrough year for Manny Ramirez, it was a tumultuous season for the Cleveland Indians. The team was scheduled to begin holding its spring training camp at a brand-new complex in Homestead, Florida, but as Hurricane Andrew swept through the southern states, the site was destroyed, relocating the Indians to an older facility in Winter Haven, Florida.

Three weeks into spring training, tragedy struck the team when two young relief pitchers were killed and a veteran starter seriously injured in a boating accident on the team's only off-day of the spring. The entire team was shattered, and it was very hard to get back to playing baseball.

It was supposed to be a happy and exciting time for the Indians. A talented group of young players, a new spring-training home, and a new major-league stadium scheduled to open in 1994 had begun to provide hope for the team, which had not been to the World Series since 1954.

Although the Indians had not enjoyed a winning season in six years, with strong performances from Albert Belle, Kenny Lofton, and Carlos Baerga, the team had shown signs of turning the corner in 1992. Even though the Indians finished in fourth place with a 76-86 record the previous season, expectations were high for 1993.

But the deaths of two teammates immediately changed everything. Even baseball would have to wait as Indians players, both young and old, first had to deal with their grief. Players on the team sought comfort and advice from their manager and each other. Twenty-four-year-old second baseman Carlos Baerga stepped forward as the team's spokesman and made himself available to his teammates as well. A native Puerto Rican, Baerga became a steadying influence and role model for many of the young Latin players.

Baerga was modest about his role with the team, but he assumed a responsible position just the same.

"I don't want to be mentioned as a leader," he told a reporter from *Sports Illustrated.* "I just like to help the Latin players. Remember, we are maybe 150 Latin players in all of Major League Baseball. We have to compete against a lot of American players. They're never going to give us everything. We have to work hard, do our jobs, and care about ourselves."

The Cleveland Indians teams that Manny has played on throughout the 1990s have contained a large number of Latin American players. In 1993, in addition to Baerga at second base, Dominican-born Felix Fermin played shortstop. Puerto Ricans Sandy Alomar, Jr., and Junior Ortiz were the catchers. Venezuelans Alvaro Espinoza and Carlos Martinez shared time at third base, Dominican Jose Mesa led the team in innings pitched, and Puerto Rican outfielder Candy Maldonado joined the team late in the season.

By 1995, Nicaraguan hero Dennis Martinez, the winningest Latin American pitcher of all time, and young Dominican hurlers Julian Tavarez and Bartolo Colon were added, as well as Venezuelan shortstop Omar Vizquel, who was traded to the Indians in 1994.

Indians general manager John Hart explained to the *Sporting News* why the team had so many Latin American stars.

"I'm not saying this to be humble, but [ethnic diversity] didn't happen by design but by accident," Hart said. "The reason we built this club the way we did is character. We judge that there's no consideration of race or language. You look at talent and you look at character. And probably in that order. Sandy Alomar, Carlos Baerga, Omar Vizquel, Jose Mesa: These are guys with great character. And great talent."

It has proven to be a formula for success for the Indians, who have been one of baseball's winningest teams in the 1990s.

"We probably have more ethnic diversity on our club than anybody else in baseball," said Hart.

While the 1993 Indians were not yet the powerhouse club the team would become, big-league prospects like Manny were providing an optimistic view of the future. By September of that year, the Indians were convinced Manny had played so well at every level that he was ready for the big leagues. But the character that Hart spoke of would become a necessary part of Manny's game for him to continue to succeed. After playing his first game at Yankee Stadium, impressing his hometown fans and new team with two home runs and a double, playing at the major-league level would become a lot tougher. He collected only five more hits the rest of the way, all of them singles, finishing his first month in the majors with a .178 average.

The 1993 Indians finished the season with a record identical (76-86) to that of the 1992 club, which wasn't all that bad considering the adversity they had overcome.

Following the season, Manny returned to the Dominican Republic, where he played winter ball for the Santiago Aguilas (Eagles) from the end of the 1993 season right up until February 1994.

He hit .315 during spring training with three home runs, and earned a spot as starting right fielder on the Indians 1994 Opening Day roster. Prior to the season, baseball statistics guru Bill James, who publishes an annual player-ratings book, said, "Ramirez is the best hitting prospect to come to the majors since Frank Thomas and Juan Gonzalez came up in 1990."

CHAPTER FIVE
Triumph and Tragedy

With the difficult but encouraging 1993 season behind them, the Indians were looking forward to the new year in a new ballpark. For nearly fifty years, the Indians had played in Cleveland Municipal Stadium, a large, cavernous arena more suited for football than baseball. The move to brand-new Jacobs Field, designed to be more of a traditional ballpark, signaled the rebirth of the Indians franchise.

The Indians had not been to the World Series in forty years and had finished at or near last place during most of the time since then, but with rising stars like Baerga, speedy outfielder Kenny Lofton, and slugger Albert Belle, many baseball people had predicted that the team's fortunes were on the brink of taking a turn.

Jacobs Field opened on April 4, 1994. The Indians defeated the Seattle Mariners 4-3 in front of an Opening Day crowd of 41,259 in what would be the first of 28 straight sold-out home games. New designated hitter/first baseman, veteran slugger Eddie Murray, hit a home run and Manny hit a run-scoring double. According to Indians manager Mike Hargrove, Murray provided counsel and advice, and served as a mentor to Manny during the 1994 season.

"From what I could gather, Eddie Murray was probably that player with Manny, as he was with a lot of the young players we had at the time," said Hargrove.

With 17 years of big-league experience, Murray had been to three World Series and hit more than 400 home runs. He was a quiet man when talking to reporters, but always a clubhouse leader with his teammates.

In addition to Murray, Dominican-born Tony Pena, a former All-Star catcher and hero to many of the young Dominican players, also joined the Indians for the 1994 season. Much like Baerga before him, Pena would be a leader and role model to the young Latin American players on the team. General manager Hart had previously spent three years managing teams in the Dominican Winter League. During his time in the Dominican Republic, Hart learned a lot about what drives the Dominican players.

"The great pride that the veteran Latin player takes in his American career, his career as a major-league player and translating that down to younger players," was why Hart brought players like Pena to Cleveland for more than just his ability as a hitter and catcher, as Hart explained to *The Sporting News*. Having Tony Pena around helped ease Manny's transition to the big leagues. Manny's locker was located next to Pena's so that the veteran catcher could advise Manny throughout the year.

Manny hit his first home run of the season on April 10 in Kansas City, and had the second two–home run game of his career, with five RBIs, the next night in California, as the Indians took an early lead in the American League's Central Division. Later in the month he hit home runs in three consecutive games from April 26-28.

By the end of the month, Manny had a .313 batting average with six home runs, second on the team only to Murray at the time, and tied Murray for the team lead with 21 RBIs.

But after his terrific first month, Manny slumped, with a .132 batting average during the month of May. Some people in the Indians organization suggested sending him back to the minors. However, Manny had the support of the most important decision maker, the team's manager, Mike Hargrove.

"The commitment to Manny has already been made," Hargrove said at the time. "Baseball is a game that lends itself to patience. If you're not patient, the chances are you'll end up in an insane asylum or quit and do something else.

"With a guy like Manny, with his tools, we were going to give him every chance in the world."

Manny also assured Hargrove that he would not let him or the team down.

"Don't worry," he said. "I'm going to come out of this."

No sooner had the month turned from May to June when Manny began to return to his early-season form, as the Indians were also beginning to fulfill their potential and appeared to be heading for the postseason (league playoffs and possibly the World Series) for the first time since 1954.

Manny played a big part in the team's success. From June 6-12 he hit .579, going 11-19 with seven runs scored, three doubles, two home runs and six RBIs, and was honored as the American League's Player of the Week.

On June 15, the Indians moved into first place. Not since 1974 had the team occupied first place this late in the season. Two days later the Indians set a team record with their 17th straight home victory, and when the one millionth fan passed through the turnstiles at Jacobs Field in the Indians 28th home game, it matched the shortest amount of time taken to reach that attendance mark.

The 17th home win was also their eighth straight overall, giving the Indians the best record in the American League (39-25). By June 19, Manny had contributed with 11 home runs and 38 RBIs.

It had been 35 years since the Indians had been considered contenders to win the American League pennant. It had been a long time since young baseball players had heroes to imitate in Cleveland. But Indians general manager John Hart said he saw that changing.

"I was driving past a field in my neighborhood, and there were about 20 kids in a pickup baseball game. About all of them wore Indians caps. It dawned on me: The kids sense what is happening here. They have stars to look up to. It's been a long time," said Hart.

Unfortunately, while the Indians were enjoying the team's first great season in decades, Major League

Baseball was embroiled in a heated labor dispute that threatened to end the season.

The players union and the owners were at odds over financial matters concerning proposed salary caps on team payrolls. While the owners were trying to control the cost of doing business, players thought a salary cap would limit their potential earnings. Lawyers on both sides of the argument met and tried to find solutions to the problem throughout the season, but failed to come up with a plan that was agreeable to both sides.

Meanwhile, baseball and the Indians kept rolling along. On July 10 the Indians were still in first place, but the Chicago White Sox had moved into a tie with them. Under a new three-division league format instituted at the start of the 1994 season, the three first-place teams would advance to the playoffs in addition to a "wild-card" entry, which would be the second-place team with the best record. In late July, the Indians slipped into second place, but still had a record good enough to qualify for the wild-card spot. The Indians and White Sox continued to jockey for first place, and as late as August 7, the two were tied again.

Five days later, on August 12, the 1994 season came to an abrupt end. Failing to reach an agreement with the owners, the players' union went on strike. When a month had passed without a settlement, acting commissioner Bud Selig, representing the owners, declared the season canceled on September 15. There would be no wild-card spot for the Indians, no long awaited, much anticipated trip to the playoffs or the

World Series. The season was simply over, with no conclusion.

With a 66-47 record, the Indians were in second place, but would have been the American League's wild-card winner.

Catcher Sandy Alomar openly wept during a television interview after the season had been officially canceled.

"I saw the light, man," Alomar said to a *New York Newsday* reporter. "That's why I was emotional. It happens. If I knew I was going to cry, and maybe look stupid, maybe I wouldn't have done it.

"The reason I was upset is that this team has been through so much. I've been through so much, with all the injuries. After five years' hard work, to end up like this...."

Although it wasn't a full season, it was still Manny's first full year in the big leagues, and despite its disheartening end, still a very productive one for the budding young star. Manny finished second behind Kansas City's Bob Hamelin in the 1994 Rookie of the Year balloting conducted by the Baseball Writers' Association of America. He also finished second among AL rookies in just about every offensive category, with 22 doubles, 17 home runs, and 60 RBIs.

"If the season wasn't stopped by the strike, I don't know if I would have won it or not," Manny told a reporter from *Baseball Weekly*. "But Hamelin deserved to win it. He had a very good year."

In the winter he returned home again to play for the Aguilas in the Dominican winter league.

Manny's teammate Tony Pena, a veteran of many Dominican Winter League seasons, explained why it was important for him to return home for the winter league even after playing in the majors from March to October.

From Rob Ruck's "Tropic of Baseball," Pena was quoted: "How could I sit out?" Pena said. "It would be like slapping the people here in the face. Besides," he added, "you've got to be crazy to play this game and I love to play this game. I just love to.

"I come back to Palo Verde as often as I can," Pena explained. "I love the land, and the people there are my real friends. I care more about what people there think of me than anywhere else. I don't want them to see me any different than I was. I would not be Tony Pena if I didn't come back."

For young ballplayers growing up on the island, the Dominican League is as important as the major leagues are to aspiring professional baseball players growing up in America.

"I wanted to be a ballplayer for as long as I can remember," Pena said. "I would fall asleep at night listening to the Aguilas play. When we made up sides, no one else wanted to catch but me. I wanted to be like Enrique Lantigua [considered one of the best Dominican catchers ever]. I made a mitt from cardboard, and my brother Ramon and I made a ball by cutting the tube of a tire into strips and wrapping it together. The bats were made from pieces of the guisama tree."

During the winter, the 38-year-old Pena made sure Manny worked hard. When he thought Manny might be taking it easy during batting practice, he insisted that Manny did "something" every time he swung the bat. He instructed Manny to go to the plate with a purpose and remain focused on whatever the particular at-bat called for.

Manny finished second in "Rookie of the Year" balloting during the strike-shortened 1994 season.

CHAPTER SIX
First Big Year

The players' strike of 1994 continued through most of 1995 spring training and threatened to cancel the 1995 season, but a court ruling in favor of the players' union put the players back on the field. In all, the strike lasted 234 days and delayed the start of the 1995 season almost a month, with Opening Day coming on April 25.

If 1994 was a year that offered hope and promise for the Indians, 1995 was the year that those possibilities would be realized. Even though he was not an everyday starter in 1994, and despite the fact that the season had been cut short, Manny had made a strong first impression and people were expecting big things from him.

"History shows us that there is at least one and normally two rookies in every crop who will wind up in Cooperstown [at the baseball Hall of Fame]," said Bill James in his 1995 player-ratings book. "My bets from the 1994 rookies: Manny Ramirez and Ryan Klesko."

"Last spring I proved to myself that if I put something in my mind, I could do it," Manny said at the beginning of the 1995 season.

It was apparent right in the first game that Manny and the Indians were on the brink of a breakthrough season. Manny had a career-high four hits, including a double and a home run with three RBIs, as the Indians defeated the Texas Rangers 11-6. Manny hit his second home run of the season the very next day.

Two weeks later, with a 3-2 win over the Kansas City Royals at Jacobs Field on May 10, the Indians

Manny reached new career highs in home runs, RBIs, and batting average, and played in his first All-Star game in 1995.

moved into first place—where the team would remain for the rest of the season.

During the month of May, Manny started to establish himself as one of baseball's premier sluggers, hitting .394 with 11 home runs, 27 RBIs, and 23 runs scored. On May 16 he hit his fifth career home run at hometown Yankee Stadium. From May 14-29, he strung together a career-high 13-game hitting streak and earned accolades from his manager, Mike Hargrove.

"Manny does everything so effortlessly, and the ball just jumps off his bat," Hargrove said. "He has the talent to hit a pitch no matter where the pitcher throws it."

Manny was also beginning to recognize and acknowledge his own ability.

"Wherever they pitch it, I hit it," he said. "I don't care if I hit it to left or to right field."

On June 3, the Indians were 23-10 with a five-game lead in their division. Manny was tied for the American League lead with a .375 batting average, and tied for second place with 12 home runs and 32 RBIs. Batting coach Charlie Manuel started calling Manny "the Baby Bull," a nickname that had previously belonged to the great Puerto Rican slugger Orlando Cepeda, because both players had become dominant power hitters at a very young age.

The Cleveland outfield, which consisted of Manny in right, Kenny Lofton, who had scored more than 100 runs in each of the last two seasons, in center, and Albert Belle, who hit more than 34 home runs while driving in more than 100 runs in each of his last three years, in left, was considered the best in baseball.

"Offensively, there's no question this may be the best outfield in the game," said general manager John Hart to *Baseball America*. "You've got the best leadoff hitter in baseball [Lofton], who is a great hitter with speed. You've got one of the premier power hitters in the game in left field, and he's also an outstanding hitter. And in Manny, you've got a guy who eventually is going to be a middle-of-the-order run producer."

With Manny's position firmly in place, he was ready to make the next big move of his life. Although he had been with the team for more than a full year, Manny had continued to live in Washington Heights during the off-season. He liked being with his family and friends and eating at his favorite restaurant, but Washington Heights was not without its problems. The neighborhood remained troubled by drug dealers and gang violence and always presented the possibility of danger.

"We thought it would be a good idea to have Manny and his family, if they wished, come to live in Cleveland," Hart said to a *New York Times* reporter. "You never know what can happen back there. We believe in Manny as a person. And we feel he has a tremendous future, so we'd like to try to protect him the best we can."

At first Manny was unhappy with the move. "It's hard to leave where you grew up," he said.

One thing that helped Manny feel better was that his mother, sister, and niece moved in with him during the season, and later teammate Julian Taverez, a fellow Dominican, became his roommate. After a while Manny came to enjoy his new surroundings in the Cleveland area, which has a Latin community of approximately 30,000. Manny even found a new favorite restaurant.

"It's different [from New York]," Manny said. "But it's safe. I don't even lock the doors of my car. It's not like where I grew up, with the drugs and the shootings."

But Manny never forgot his old hometown of Washington Heights and how important it was for him. During the season, he sent fifty pairs of spikes and batting gloves to his old high-school team.

"Manny's a legend around here," his high-school coach, Steve Mandl said to a *New York Times* reporter. "I can talk to my kids all about goals and that they can make it by hard work, but unless they can see it first-hand, it doesn't have the same impact. But Manny's something tangible. They all know him. Know what he had to do to get where he is. He's something for them to grasp. He's one of them."

Manny's legend continued to grow as the 1995 season progressed. On July 6, he hit his 17th and 18th home runs of the season with 4 RBIs in an 8-1 victory over Seattle. Five days later he played in his first All-Star Game, being selected as a reserve by American League manager Buck Showalter. Manny was one of six Indians to make the team.

At the time of the All-Star break, the Indians had the best record in baseball and led the league in batting average, hits, total bases, home runs and slugging percentage. The pitching staff led the league in earned run average and shutout saves, and had allowed the fewest walks.

On August 4, Manny hit his first career grand slam against the Chicago White Sox, and equaled his

"Wherever they pitch it, I hit it. I don't care if I hit it to left or right field."

career-best with five RBIs in the game. The Indians were 18 1/2 games ahead of second-place Kansas City and kept on rolling, clinching the division on September 8 and eventually winning the Central Division by 30 games. Manny finished the season with a .308 batting average, 31 home runs and 107 RBIs, and at 23, became the twenty-fifth player ever and the second-youngest Cleveland Indian to collect 30 homers and 100 RBIs in a season.

At 100-44 (.694), the Indians finished the season with their best record since 1954.

"People say that it is about time we're winning," Hargrove said to *Baseball Weekly* earlier in the season. "I'm glad they're saying it. I feel the same way."

The fans in Cleveland were delirious with delight. It had been two generations since baseball had provided them with this much excitement. While most of the rest of the teams in the majors were still struggling to win fans back in the year following the strike, every game at Jacobs Field since June 12 had been sold out. The Indians average attendance of 39,965 was 61.5 percent above the major-league average.

The players also knew they were part of something special.

"This is a completely different city," said pitcher Dennis Martinez. "Before, no one wanted to play in Cleveland. You talk to a lot of players now and they would like to play here. The park has a lot to do with it. The old stadium was a bad place to be. You went there and felt like you were going to injure yourself. It was a park that gave you stress. You want to go to a baseball game and relax and eat popcorn and peanuts. You don't want to go to the park and have stress."

Although Manny did not have a great series, the Indians made easy work of the American League Eastern Division champion Boston Red Sox with a three-game sweep in the first round, the best-of-five league playoffs.

Manny circles the bases after hitting his first World Series home run in 1995.

The Indians advanced to the American League Championship series, where they would meet the Seattle Mariners, who had just defeated the New York Yankees, the league's first wild-card playoff team under the new division format. Manny had two home runs in the series with a .286 average as the Indians moved passed Seattle four games to two in the best-of-seven series. Meanwhile, the Atlanta Braves had defeated Colorado and Cincinnati in the National League playoffs to meet Cleveland in the World Series.

The Braves had become baseball's dominant National League team during the 1990s, mostly because of an unparalleled pitching staff led by Greg Maddux, who later would be named the Cy Young Award winner as the league's best pitcher—the fourth straight year he had won the award. Teammate Tom Glavine was the last man to win the award before Maddux, giving the Braves five consecutive Cy Young awards.

Atlanta's pitching proved too much for the Indians to handle. Batting a mere .179 as a team, the Indians dream season came to an end as they lost the Series four games to two.

Despite the Series loss, 1995 will always be remembered as the year the Indians' fortunes finally took a turn for the better. It was also the year that Manny established himself as one of the league's star players, winning his first Silver Slugger Award and being named to *The Sporting News* All-Star team.

The only problem with the kind of success Manny had enjoyed was maintaining the same high standards he had now set for himself.

CHAPTER SEVEN
Keeping Pace With Himself

Even though the Indians had finally enjoyed success after so many years of failure, and could fly an American League championship flag over Jacobs Field, there was a burning desire to accomplish more. Most players and teams would be happy with the kind of season the Indians had had in 1995, but for the Indians, just making it to the World Series was not enough. Winning had now become part of the Indians routine, something that the players, fans, and ownership not only looked forward to but expected.

The team had enjoyed tremendous success since the opening of Jacobs Field, and several months before the opening of the 1996 season, the Indians had sold every ticket to every home game.

With a renewed commitment to winning, the team's owners entered the free-agent market, signing veteran pitcher Jack McDowell. They also acquired designated hitter Julio Franco, another Dominican legend with 15 years in the big leagues.

"We could have put the money in the bank," said general manger John Hart. "But [owner] Dick Jacobs kept saying, 'This city is a baseball treasure, and because of that we have to do whatever we can to win.'"

Manny's contract was also renewed at this time, keeping him signed with Cleveland through the year 2000. In addition to Manny, the Indians renewed the contracts of several other players, ensuring that most of the team would be together for at least the next few years.

"What we've done is keep our entire team, plus add Jack and a great hitter in Julio Franco," Hart said. "These fans in Cleveland deserve everything we can give them."

Although the Indians got off to slow start (losing the first three games of the season), they got back in first place on April 13 with a 14-2 victory at Boston. The team would remain there for the rest of the season.

On April 21, Manny hit two home runs in a game for the fifth time in his career in an 11-7 victory over Boston that kept the Indians tied for first place with the Chicago White Sox. Throughout the season, the White Sox followed close behind in the Central Division race, trailing by just two games at the All-Star break.

Manny hit in 15 straight games from June 29-July 16, with ten doubles, three home runs and 14 RBIs during the streak, and heated up with the summer, hitting .351 in July and .358 in August.

The Indians went 47-27 during the second half, with a 19-7 record in September, pulling away from the White Sox. They eventually clinched their division for the second consecutive season, $14^{1}/2$ games in front of Chicago, with the best record in the majors for the second year in a row. It was also the second consecutive season that the Indians led the American League in batting (.293) and earned run average (4.34). To put in perspective how far the Indians had come, it had been nearly forty years since a team had led its league in batting and ERA for two consecutive seasons. In just a few short years, the Indians had become one of baseball's most dominant teams.

Manny reached new career highs in 1996 with 170 hits, 45 doubles, 33 home runs, 112 RBIs, 94 runs, and 85 walks, while also playing in a career-high 152 games. Manny, Albert Belle, and Jim Thome became the first group of three Indians to each have more than 30 homers and 100 RBIs in the same season, and the third such group in American League history.

Riding a full head of steam into the playoffs, the Indians appeared headed for their second straight

Manny continued to improve his single-season career highs in 1996.

World Series, but would first meet the wild-card Baltimore Orioles in the opening round of the playoffs.

The division series got off to a bad start for the Indians, when Baltimore's Brady Anderson led off the first game in the best-of-five series with a home run. The Orioles won the first two games and the Indians never recovered, eventually losing three games to one.

For his part, Manny played very well in the division series, with a .375 average and a team-high four extra-base hits including two home runs. But the loss was disappointing for Manny and the Indians, who would only have been satisfied by winning the World Series. As early as April, winning the World Series had been the team's goal.

"Until you've won a World Series and have that ring on your finger, you aren't fulfilled," Albert Belle told *Baseball America* in the beginning of the season. "We remember losing to the Braves. How can we forget it? I want to know what it's like to be standing at the end."

If Albert Belle was going to know what it feels like to be standing at the end, it wasn't going to be in a Cleveland uniform. The business of baseball had become much different from previous decades, and the Indians' quest to return to the World Series in 1997 would be made with a decidedly different cast of characters.

Although the Indians were the two-time defending American League Central Division champions, most of the players involved in the team's dramatic turnaround during the past couple of years had departed before the start of the new season. In addition to Albert Belle, who left the Indians to sign a $10 million-a-year contract with the Chicago White Sox, gone were former clubhouse leader Carlos Baerga and star center fielder Kenny Lofton, as well as Eddie Murray, Dennis Martinez, and others. Only 11 players from the 1995 American League Champion team were on the Indians' Opening Day roster, and only 12 from 1996 had returned.

"Welcome to baseball in the 90s," said general manager John Hart.

New in 1997 were perennial National League All-Star third baseman Matt Williams, speedy center fielder Marquis Grissom, and legendary Dominican infielder Tony Fernandez.

Returning veteran pitcher Orel Hershiser was pleased with the team's new look.

"I thought our 1996 team was better than our 1995 team, and our 1997 team may be even better than 1996," Hershiser said.

The new Indians did not exactly burst out of the starting blocks, and were just 12-13 at the end of the 1997 season's first month. But the team still remained at or near first place through May, and by June 5 had captured the lead for good.

Manny, continuing to improve, was on his way to his best season yet. He hit the fifth grand slam of his career off New York Yankees pitcher Graeme Lloyd on June 21 in 13-4 drubbing of the Yankees at Jacobs Field. The homer was one of four hits for Manny, as he drove in a career-high six runs and was named Player of the Week for June 16-22. Manny hit another grand slam two weeks later on July 6, tying him for third-most in team history.

The Indians hosted the 68th All-Star Game at Jacobs Field, and teammate Sandy Alomar, Jr., was named the game's Most Valuable Player.

Manny collected the 500th hit of his career on July 13 and his 100th home run on August 8. The Indians maintained their lead over second-place Chicago, eventually clinching their third straight division title on September 23.

Manny finished the season with a new career-high batting average of .328, with 40 doubles, 26 home runs and 88 RBIs. His 184 hits were also the most he had ever accumulated in a season, as he batted in the third and fourth spot in the order most of the year.

The World Series matched the Indians against the National League champion Florida Marlins, the first wild-card team ever to reach the Series. The Marlins defeated Western Division winner San Francisco in the first round and surprised reigning World Champion Atlanta in the League Championship Series.

Outside Pro Player stadium in Miami, there was a Latin flavor to the pregame atmosphere. Chef Pepin from the Spanish TV station Univision was preparing a free sampling of his paella, and salsa music was broadcast from a pair of remote stations. Cuban pitcher Livan Hernandez, who had struck out 15 Braves during his last start in game five of the National League Championship Series, would start game one for the Marlins.

The Indians scored the game's first run in the top of the first inning, but the Marlins answered with

Known primarily for his slugging, Manny has worked hard at becoming one of the game's solid outfielders and has been a mainstay in right field for Cleveland throughout his career.

Manny collected 184 hits in 1997 and reached a new career high .328 batting average.

a run in the third, four more in the fourth and two in the fifth. Manny hit a solo homer in the sixth, as did teammate Jim Thome in the seventh, but the Marlins held on for a 7-4 win.

Cleveland evened the Series with a 6-1 win in game two, and the Series moved back to Cleveland. But the Marlins took a two-games-to-one lead, outslugging the Indians 14-11 in game three. Manny hit his second home run of the Series in a 10-3 game four win, as Cleveland once again evened the Series. The Marlins edged the Indians 8-7 in game five, despite a ninth-inning, three-run rally by the Indians.

The Indians were in a must-win situation when the Series moved back to Miami for the final two games. Cleveland forced a seventh game as Manny drove in

two runs with a pair of sacrifice flies in a 4-1 Indians victory. The seesaw battle would be resolved in an exciting 11-inning seventh game.

The Indians had a 2-0 lead after seven innings, but Marlins third baseman Bobby Bonilla hit a solo home run in the bottom of the inning and second baseman Craig Counsell tied the game with a sacrifice fly in the bottom of the ninth.

Finally, in the bottom of the 11th, the Marlins won the game and the Series on an RBI single by shortstop Edgar Rentaria, only the fourth Colombian-born major-leaguer.

It was a thrilling Series that could have gone either way, but the loss was still terribly disappointing to an Indians team that had set the World Series Championship as its ultimate goal.

Manny's four home runs in the playoffs and World Series moved him into first place on the Indians postseason list. In the end, it was another fine season for Manny and the Indians, but the hunt for that elusive World Series title would have to wait yet another year.

CHAPTER EIGHT
The Year of the Home Run

It will forever be remembered as the year of the home run. Mark McGwire and Sammy Sosa's race to Roger Maris's single-season home run record overshadowed just about everything else that happened in baseball in 1998.

Home runs aside, it was still a very eventful year. Two new teams were added to the major-league roster, the Arizona Diamondbacks in the National League and the Tampa Bay Devil Rays in the American League. The New York Yankees got off to a great start and ended the season with one of the best records in the history of the game. Along the way Yankees pitcher David Wells threw the 15th perfect game in major league history and the first in four years. Iron man Cal Ripken's streak of consecutive games played finally came to an end, and Bud Selig, who had been baseball's interim acting Commissioner for six years, was finally named as actual Commissioner of Baseball. The game enjoyed increased popularity, as per-game attendance rose to 29,000, up four percent from 1997 and the third-highest figure ever. The San Francisco Giants, Chicago Cubs, and New York Mets were engaged in a three-way race for the National League wild card until the last day of the season, with the Giants and Cubs staging a one-game playoff to decide the eventual winner. Cuban pitcher Orlando "El Duque" Hernandez, half-brother of 1997 World Series hero Livan Hernandez, signed with the Yankees after defecting from Cuba in a dramatic late-night departure by boat, heralding things to come.

For the Indians, it was business as usual. Once again, nothing but a World Series Championship would do. Once again they grabbed control of the Central Division early, this time taking first place on Opening Day and holding it for the remainder of the season.

Manny was one of 20 Latin players named to the 1998 All-Star game.

More Latin players continued to exert their influence on the game. So many Latin players were named to the 1998 All-Star Game that Venezuelan slugger, Andres Galarraga, the Atlanta Braves first baseman, suggested a different kind of midseason classic.

"We have so many Latin guys we could have an All-Star Game against the American guys,"

Galarraga told a *New York Times* reporter. "We can get a good game like that. All Americans against all Latins."

On the 1998 All-Star rosters there were 20 Latins, including Manny, compared to 14 the year before and 18 the year before that.

"It makes me proud," said Colorado Rockies third baseman Vinny Castilla of Mexico, "because every Latin player who comes here has difficulties with the language, has different cultures. I give myself and other players a lot of credit to come here and have success because it wasn't easy for me to come here and learn the language and adjust to life in the United States. It makes me feel proud. We work so hard to be where we are."

Moises Alou, a Dominican outfielder for the Houston Astros and member of one of Major League Baseball's first Dominican families, was impressed with the ever-growing number of Dominican major-leaguers and the continued growth of the game in Latin American countries.

"They see the results of the Sammy Sosas, the Raul Mondesis, the Juan Gonzalezes," Alou said, "plus they're building beautiful facilities. In the Dominican Republic, the Diamondbacks have a complex where I haven't seen a major-league ballpark with grass like that."

At the season's midway point, Manny was hitting .323 with 11 home runs and 62 RBIs, and he was named to the All-Star team for the second time in his career. He poured it on during the second half, especially late in the season. While "Big Mac" and "Sammy" were grabbing most of the headlines, Manny was also becoming one of the game's slugging elite. On September 15, Manny hit three homers in a game for the first time in his career. The next night he hit another home run in his first at bat of the game, tying the major-league record for home runs in consecutive at bats. When he blasted one more later in the game, he equaled another major-league mark with five homers during a two-game stretch. His record-pace tear continued with another home run on September 17 and two more on September 19, giving him eight multi–home run games on the season and 14 for his career. He was selected as the obvious choice for Player of the Week after driving eight balls out of the park from September 14-20.

Meanwhile, the Indians clinched the AL Central for the fourth consecutive season, then made relatively easy work of the Boston Red Sox in the American League division series, winning three games to one. It was on to New York and the powerful Yankees, who had won 114 regular season games, for the American League Championship Series.

Manny had always performed well in front of his hometown fans in New York, and he used the playoff stage to show the rest of the country what fans in Cleveland already knew.

"He is in front of his home crowd," said Indians shortstop Omar Vizquel. "I'm sure the atmosphere and the crowd really gets him pumped up. It has to."

Adding to his numbers as postseason home run leader among active players, Manny clubbed his 12th and 13th in the playoffs against the Yankees. But the Yankees left the Indians on the brink of elimination after a game five win left them up three games to two.

"We all need to do what we can," Manny said after the loss.

Unfortunately for the Indians, the eventual World Champion 1998 Yankees proved too tough for any team to match, and brought the Indians' World Series hopes to an end in six games.

Way back on the first day of spring training, first baseman Jim Thome passed out T-shirts to his team-

Third base coach Jeff Newman congratulates Manny after he hit one of his post-season home runs.

mates that read *It don't mean a thing till we get the ring.* Four fantastic seasons had yielded four division titles in a row, and two World Series appearances. Although the Indians of the 90s were a far cry from the perennial losing teams of the past, they had still yet to obtain any World Series rings.

For Manny, 1998 was a breakthrough year in which he established himself as one of baseball's premier sluggers. He won The Tribe Man of the Year Award, given to the Indians team MVP, having yet again the best year of his career. His batting average (.294) dipped below .300 for the first time since his rookie year of 1994, but he set new career marks with 45 home runs, 145 RBIs, and 108 runs scored, and finished sixth in American League MVP voting.

CHAPTER NINE
Top Run Producer

In 1997, a *Baseball America* article predicted that Manny Ramirez might possibly be the American League's Most Valuable Player in the year 2000. After four seasons of consistent and continual improvement, Manny almost arrived there ahead of schedule, putting together a dream season in 1999.

Right from the start of the season, Manny picked up where he left off in 1998 and began driving in runs at a record pace that had people discussing the possibility of Manny breaking Hack Wilson's 69-year-old record of 190 RBIs in a season. With the season barely six weeks old, Manny had already driven in 42 runs as the Indians moved out to a 5$\frac{1}{2}$ game lead over the second-place White Sox in the AL Central.

Manny quietly went about his business, seldom granting interviews, preferring to let his play on the field speak for itself. However, in May, he and his Indians teammates spoke with *USA Today Baseball Weekly* reporter Bob Nightengale.

"He's the most unassuming guy you'd ever want to meet," said Indians catcher Sandy Alomar, Jr. "People don't realize how humble he is."

In the same story, Manny explained his philosophy.

"I just want to play baseball," he said. "That's it. I don't care if anybody knows who I am, or what people think of me. I just want to stay quiet and relaxed."

While he does not spend a lot of time talking to reporters, with his teammates he is loose and speaks freely, most often offering words of encouragement and support.

"He walks around in here and makes everybody believe they're as good as him. He wants everybody to think they can hit like him," added Alomar.

The 1999 season in Cleveland bore a close resemblance to the previous four. For the fifth straight year, the Indians had grabbed early control of their division and had their sights set on the World Series. On May 7, the Indians came back from an eight-run deficit in a game against the Tampa Bay Devil Rays, scoring 18 runs in the last three innings of a 20-11 win that served to warn the rest of the league about the power of their lineup.

"I've never seen anything like it," Indians third baseman Travis Fryman told *USA Today Baseball Weekly*. "But I've never seen anything like this team, either. I think we're the most explosive team in baseball. When it comes to offensive potency, this team is unmatched."

The Indians were also unmatched when it came to packing the stadium, selling out every home game since June 12, 1995 through the 1999 season, a total of 308 games.

After the 20-11 beating, Tampa Bay Devil Rays manager Chuck Lamar called the Indians "the model franchise for all of baseball."

From 1995 through 1999, the Indians have held on to first place in the American League Central more than 90 percent of the time. Going into the 1999 season, manager Mike Hargrove said the team's goal was to win 100 games and the World Series.

"Some people took that as being arrogant by saying that," Hargrove later told *Baseball Weekly.* "I didn't say that we would win 100 games and the World Series. I said it was our goal. It was a challenge to our team.

"Not one guy griped and moaned about the added pressure. They responded. A lot of teams don't understand what they're trying to accomplish. This one does."

At the All-Star break, the Indians were on track to reach Hargrove's goals, in first place by 13 games in front of second-place Chicago.

In addition to driving in more runs (165) than anyone in the last 61 years, Manny finished fourth in the American League with 131 runs scored in 1999.

Manny earned his third selection to the All-Star Game. He had already hit 25 home runs with an incredible 96 runs batted in and a .333 batting average.

A week later he revealed to an *Arizona Republic* reporter that he was quietly focusing on the RBI record.

"One of the big reasons I don't like to do many interviews is that I want to focus all my energies and concentrate fully on the RBI record," Manny said. "I want to give my all for that record. I know I have a chance this year, and who knows, I may never be in this position again."

Manny missed six games during the season, and by late September it appeared he would not reach Hack Wilson's record of 190 RBIs in one season. However, Manny would pass 160, which no player had done in 61 years.

"Manny is absolutely amazing," said manager Hargrove. "One hundred and sixty RBIs? If you drive in 70 runs in a year people talk about that as a good offensive year. And here Manny has more than doubled that. What he's done in two years is a career for most people."

Manny would finish the season with 165, bringing his two-year total to 310. Manny drove in more runs in a season than anyone since Jimmie Foxx knocked in 175 in 1938, and his new career high for a season is more than Hall of Famers Ted Williams (159), Joe DiMaggio (155), Ty Cobb (144), Willie Mays (141), or Hank Aaron (132) ever reached.

"My goal," Manny said, "is to get 90 or 100 RBIs in a season, and if I get more than that I'm even more happy. I'm just getting the right hits at the right time," he added. "Kenny [Lofton], Omar [Vizquel] and Robbie [Alomar] are getting on base, but if I don't get the hits at the right time, they're not going to come home."

Toward the end of the season, players, reporters, and fans began speculating about Manny being named the American League's MVP.

"Manny is MVP," said Kenny Lofton. "If people don't vote for him it's a shame. Guys need to write about him. He deserves MVP and that's the bottom line."

The Indians clinched the AL Central for the fifth straight season, but made an early exit from the playoffs when they were upset by the Boston Red Sox, who came from being down 2-0 in the best-of-five series to come back and win three in a row. Once again it was a bitter pill for the Indians to swallow. Another season of high expectations had ended in frustration.

"We had one goal this year, to get to the World Series and win," said Sandy Alomar, Jr., echoing a familiar theme. "We've been saying that every year, and it seems like the same story every year. It's disappointing."

In spite of the loss, it was a brilliant season for Manny, perhaps his most brilliant, and a tough act to follow. Only eight men have driven in more runs in a season than Manny's 165. All of them are in the Hall of Fame.

Mike Hargrove said he'd never seen another player that reminds him of Manny.

"I think that what you see out of Manny are qualities that you see out of all superstar players, a natural athletic ability and an ability to play the game at a level nobody else can, both mentally and physically. It's one of those things that you see on the surface, that things come easy to Manny as far as hitting but, what you don't see, below the surface, is the absolute great work ethic and work habits that he has to allow his ability to work in those situations. He works very hard at being a good player," said Hargrove.

But sadly, for Manny, it was not enough to win him the 1999 MVP award. That went to Ivan Rodriguez, the Puerto Rican–born catcher for the Texas Rangers. Manny finished tied for third in the balloting with his teammate, Roberto Alomar. Yet 1999 was not without its rewards. Manny did become the first recipient of the Hank Aaron Award for the American League. This new award is given to the hitter in each league with the most combined hits, home runs, and RBIs. Manny won that award easily. He was also voted to the Associated Press Major League All-Star team.

It's a long way from Santo Domingo in the Dominican Republic to Cooperstown, New York, but after what Manny has accomplished during six full seasons in the majors, anything seems possible.

CHRONOLOGY

1972 Born May 30, in Santo Domingo, Dominican Republic

1985 Family moved to New York City

1991 Named "high school player of the year." Selected 13th overall in the major-league free agent draft by the Cleveland Indians. Named Appalachian League's Most Valuable Player and top prospect

1992 Promoted to Kinston Class-A Carolina League

1993 Named to Eastern League post-season All-Star team; Named Baseball America's "Minor-League Player of the Year." Made major-league debut for Cleveland at Minnesota

1994 Earned spot on opening day roster; finished second in "Rookie of the Year" balloting

1995 Played in first All-Star game; won Silver Slugger Award; named to *Sporting News'* All-Star team; played in first World Series

1997 Returned to World Series

1998 Hit 45 home runs and 145 RBIs

1999 Set new career mark with 165 RBIs, the highest single-season mark in 61 years; voted to the Associated Press Major League All-Star team

MAJOR-LEAGUE STATS

Year	Team	G	AB	R	H	HR	RBI	BB	AVG
1993	CLE	22	53	5	9	2	5	2	.170
1994	CLE	91	290	51	78	17	60	42	.269
1995	CLE	137	484	85	149	31	107	75	.308
1996	CLE	152	550	94	170	33	112	85	.309
1997	CLE	150	561	99	184	26	88	79	.328
1998	CLE	150	571	108	168	45	145	76	.294
1999	CLE	147	522	131	174	44	165	96	.333
Total		849	3031	573	932	198	682	455	.307

INDEX

Alomar, Roberto 61

Alomar Jr., Sandy 21, 22, 29, 45, 56, 60

Anderson, Brady 44

Baerga, Carlos 21, 22, 24, 45

Belle, Albert 43, 44

Castilla, Vinny 52

Cepeda, Orlando 34

DeLucca, Joe 17

Franco, Julio 42

Galarraga, Andres 51

Hargrove, Mike 12, 24, 26, 58, 60

Hart, John 21, 27, 35, 41

Hershiser, Orel 45

Klesko, Ryan 32

Gonzalez, Juan 23

Gonzalez, Ralph 6, 7

Hernandez, Livan 50

Hernandez, Orlando 50

Lamar, Chuck 57

Lloyd, Graeme 45

Lofton, Kenny 24, 34, 45

Maddux, Greg 40

Maldonado, Greg 40

Mandl, Steve 36

Manual, Charlie 34

Martinez, Dennis 21, 38, 45

McDowell, Jack 41

McGwire, Mark 50

Murray, Eddie 25, 45

Peña, Tony 25, 30

Perez, Melido 8

Ramirez, Manny

     birth of 9

     major league debut 5

     minor leagues 17–20

     moves to U.S. 13

     parents 13

     World Series 46–49

Rodriguez, Ivan 61

Selig, Bud 28

Showalter, Buck 36

Sosa, Pedro 7

Sosa, Sammy 50

Thome, Jim 43

Virgil, Ozzie 11, 22

Vizquel, Omar 53

Wells, David 50